# 24 Hours
# to Change
# Your Life.

# Contents

| | |
|---|---|
| Introduction | 3 |
| Plan Your Long-Term Goals | 4 |
| Rid Your Life of Negativity | 8 |
| Ditch Your Toxic Friend | 12 |
| Leave Your Partner | 16 |
| Revamp Your Image | 20 |
| Kickstart an Exercise Regime | 24 |
| Quit Smoking | 28 |
| Spring Clean Your Social Media | 32 |
| Have a Digital Detox | 36 |
| Meet the Love of Your Life | 40 |
| Make Your Peace with Someone | 44 |
| Plan a Family | 48 |
| Create a Budget | 52 |
| Buy a New Home | 56 |
| Declutter Your House | 60 |
| Overcome a Fear | 64 |
| Reboot Your Diet | 68 |
| Give a Little, Gain a Lot | 72 |
| Plan a Dream Trip | 76 |
| Change Your Sleep Habits | 80 |
| Go Green | 84 |
| Quit Your Job | 88 |
| Share a Problem | 92 |

# Introduction

Same-day delivery. Instant replies to emails. Web pages that load in a flash.

If we don't get things easy and fast, we get frustrated. Making changes to the way we live our life is no exception. Once you get an idea in your head, do you want to wait or do you want to get on with it straight away (preferably bypassing any hard work)? Sadly, the latter is but a delicious dream.

We know that in the real world, change takes time and preparation, especially if you want to do it properly. This book *won't* show you how to instantly change your life, but it *will* show you how to make the best use of 24 hours – kickstarting big life changes and setting yourself up for success. Whether you want to really shake it up and quit your job or simply want to eat more healthily, you'll discover how to cast procrastination aside and get on with it. No more excuses, no more dithering – this book will give you the motivation and energy you need to change your life for the better.

# Plan Your Long-Term Goals

It's easy to drift along hoping that what you want will just end up in your lap. Take the initiative and plan, plan, plan.

What better way to start a book about change than with goal-setting? You don't have to wait until New Year to think of your long-term goals and it's not about setting unrealistic expectations for yourself either. You can start small and then think big (if you wish to).

## GOALS

- Map out where you want to be and what you want to be doing in 5, 10, 20 years' time.
- Know what action plans you can put in place now to achieve your long-term goals.
- Stick to your plan!

### GETTING STARTED

Easy. All you need is a pen, paper and some thinking time. If a brand-new unicorn notebook helps, get one. Long-term plans are serious stuff but if you relax and enjoy the planning process it will be more productive. Don't think too hard initially – just start getting your thoughts down on paper. The more you write, the more the ideas will flow.

### WHAT'S IMPORTANT TO YOU?

Think about what motivates you. Is it helping other people? Making lots of money? Are you someone who needs to be creative? Your goals should be about fulfilling these, whether it be through work or your personal life. If you're doing something you enjoy, you're more likely to put your all into it. The feeling that you're meeting your core needs and being true to your values is incredibly important for your emotional well-being. Don't compromise your long-term plans by letting others dictate them or by focusing on the dreaded 'should' word.

### WRITE A LETTER FROM YOUR FUTURE SELF

If you're having trouble thinking about what your long-term goals are, write a letter to yourself from the 80-year-old you. Visualise looking back on your life. What did you do and achieve? What were you most proud of? What brought you the greatest happiness? This process will highlight what's important to you so use the answers to define your goals and what you need to do to get there.

### HOW TO GET THERE

Did you know that writing your goals down has been proven to make you more likely to achieve them? Break your goals down into the actions you need to take to move yourself one step closer. They can be big action points (e.g. enrol on a degree course) or much smaller (e.g. sign-up to a job website). The important thing is that each action is realistic and achievable – being able to tick them off as you go will give you a huge sense of achievement, plus the motivation to keep heading towards the ultimate prize. Mapping out your plan will reduce stress and kick procrastination into touch.

## DREAM BIG ... BUT KEEP IT REAL

Don't be afraid to dream big. Those dreams may spark ideas you've not considered before. However, if you're 42 there's no point making a plan to become an Olympic gymnast – sadly, some things are out of the reach no matter how much self-belief you have! So be realistic about your goals and save those thoughts of a duet with Bradley Cooper for your daydreams.

## STICK AT IT

Refer back to your goals regularly so that you don't forget them (easy to do when the rest of life gets in the way) and you can track your progress. Remember though that wants and desires (and you!) can change so don't feel you can't adjust your plans. Life has the habit of throwing up unexpected opportunities, meaning that your path isn't always set in stone. Rethink, adjust and keep moving forward.

# Rid Your Life of Negativity

To make rapid changes to your life, you need to be driven by a can-do attitude. Inject positivity into your thinking and watch the transformation.

Your brain forges pathways based on experiences. Every time you think negatively in reaction to something, you're confirming and strengthening those connections. Negativity will then repeat itself in similar situations. This bad habit can become engrained, but you can start making small changes to introduce new ways of thinking. Habits take around three months to change, but with perseverance you'll get there.

## GOALS

- Challenge the bad habits your brain has formed.
- Replace negative thoughts with positive, life-affirming alternatives.
- Use positive thinking to facilitate successful change in your life.

## SWITCH YOUR THOUGHTS

To change the way you feel, you must change the way you think. Be aware of your thoughts and how they affect you. If you're mindful of your thoughts you can catch them before they run away and spiral into negativity. When you hear "I can't do this, it's going to be a disaster", stop, and consciously replace it with "I *can* do this, it's hard but I *can* do it". The more you tell yourself that you '*can*', the more your brain is rewired, allowing you to instinctively think positively.

## START A GRATITUDE JOURNAL

We're often so busy worrying that we forget to stop and appreciate the positive. A gratitude journal is a great way to acknowledge the joys of life and change your mindset. Set aside time to write every day. It could be three things that made you happy that day. Or you could use these prompts to help aid your thinking:

• Something you're looking forward to.

• Who inspired you today?

• An act of kindness someone showed you.

• What can you see out of your window that you're grateful for?

Gratitude helps us see the fullness of life. Keeping a gratitude journal lowers stress levels and brings a sense of calm, a new perspective and clarity. You can also use the journal to reflect on past experiences and thoughts.

## POSITIVE AFFIRMATIONS

These could be statements that encourage you to think differently and reprogramme your brain. Gather together some affirmations that mean something to you or a situation you're in (the internet is a great place to find them if you aren't ready to write your own). Affirmations should always be in the present tense, e.g. "I love my body", "Today is a great day" or "I'm on the road to changing my life". If you feel uncomfortable saying the affirmation, shout it out loud! The more you say it, the less uncomfortable you'll start to feel. Repetition is key so say your affirmations several times a day or stick post-its up around your home in places you'll see them frequently.

## VISUALISE SUCCESS

Your brain doesn't know the difference between reality and imagination – this means you can trick it! As with positive affirmations, if you tell yourself something enough you can make your brain believe it. Visually imagining success is very powerful and, like physically writing down your goals, has been shown to increase your chances of achieving what you want. Think of the changes you would like to make in your life and imagine a moment that demonstrates success. For example, if you want to quit smoking, visualise someone offering you a cigarette and you saying – without hesitation – "No thanks, I don't smoke". Now imagine how good that would feel! This will encourage you to make those important changes without fear of failure.

# Ditch Your Toxic Friend

They don't have your interests at heart, they're selfish, they're rude, they try to control you and they criticise you – your friendship is an emotional rollercoaster.

A toxic friendship is an incredibly stressful relationship to maintain. The good news is that it's very quick to take the first steps to stamp it out. The negative effects of a toxic friendship can leave you vulnerable to higher blood pressure, depression and anxiety. So it's crucial to end the relationship before it gets any worse. A genuine friendship has a completely different effect – in fact, studies have shown that having a solid and supportive friendship group can actually increase your life expectancy.

## GOALS

- Erase from your life any so-called friends who make you utterly miserable. You're worth so much more than that.
- Free up your time to focus on a supportive friendship group that is good for your soul.
- Feel the weight of a toxic friendship lift off your shoulders and the stress melt away.

### SAY GOODBYE FOR GOOD

If someone is unhealthy for you, how can you declutter them from your life as painlessly as possible? When you're kind-hearted and care about others, it's hard to tell someone that you don't want them around anymore, even if they're an unpleasant person. Think about how they treat you and how that makes you feel – this will remind you that you don't owe them a detailed explanation. Be honest and keep it to the point. If you don't feel able to explicitly tell them you don't want to see them, you can gradually distance yourself. Keep yourself busy elsewhere with other friends and let time do the work.

## THEY WON'T LEAVE ME ALONE!

Don't expect the person to back off immediately. After all, they probably can't understand why you wouldn't want a friend as wonderful as them! Distancing yourself can take time but being patient and firm will speed the process along. Block them on social media, your phone and email. Make it as hard as possible for them to contact you. Delete any emails and social media posts that connect you. Consider avoiding those places you know they might turn up (not forever), or at least go there with other friends for support.

Resist the urge to re-engage on any level. They may try to 'win' you back or try to punish you by making your life difficult. Whatever they do and however angry it makes you feel, ignore it and let it wash over you. Ditching a toxic friend is a tough thing to do, but it's time to stop letting them control your life.

## PUT YOURSELF FIRST

When you're used to trying to please other people, ditching a friend is hard, but it needs to be done for your own physical and emotional well-being. Focus on the friends who bring stability and happiness to your life – the ones who love you for who you are. Reclaim all the time and energy you've been expending on toxic friends and channel it into the people whose friendships you truly value. With a trusted support network comes the security and calmness of mind that you deserve. Take half an hour to text or call good friends you've lost touch with and bring their light back into your life.

# Leave Your Partner

If it's time to move on, there are ways to do it kindly and honestly so you can both walk away with heads held high.

Breaking up is hard to do, no doubt about it. There are so many confusing thoughts and high-octane emotions involved. Are you doing the right thing? Will you manage alone? You can't avoid hurt feelings but there are ways to ensure you can move forward in a positive frame of mind, knowing you've done the right thing.

## GOALS

- Prepare yourself for the big step of ending a romantic relationship.
- Behave in a way that minimises the impact on both of you.
- Get through the break-up intact.

## CHOOSE THE RIGHT TIME AND PLACE

It's tempting to postpone a break-up conversation because you're dreading it – but only postpone it until the right time. Choose a moment with no distractions so you can both focus on what's being said. You'll be imagining all kinds of scenarios for how the conversation will play out but try to rein in your imagination. If you approach it well, the result may be less stressful than you think. Preparation is key, so know what you want to say and anticipate the responses your partner might give.

Launch straight into the conversation rather than sandwich it in small talk. A good way to start the conversation is to say, "I know what I'm about to say might not be easy to hear, but it's really important that we talk about this." Unless you're living on opposite sides of the world, always do it in person. Breaking up by text or email may seem the easy option if you're feeling anxious, but have some respect for the other person – and for yourself.

## CUSHION THE BLOW

When delivering bad news, you need to be gentle to minimise the damage; not so gentle that the message gets lost in the padding, but sensitive nonetheless. Is there an angle you can take that draws in something positive (without being patronising)? The break-up shouldn't overshadow the good memories you've built together, so acknowledge those parts of the relationship that were good. Remember, honesty is the best policy. But also remember that you can be honest without being brutal.

It's important to avoid trying to make the other person feel better – you can't be a part of their ongoing support network. Downshifting your relationship to friendship is also problematic; whilst it may feel you're being kinder, it only causes uncertainty, false hopes and the risk of more hurt in the future.

## MOVING FORWARD

Aim to break off the relationship as cleanly as possible. Try to cut off contact for a while to let emotions settle. This will give your partner the signal that you were serious and that things have changed permanently.

It's normal to feel sad, even if you're the one who ended the relationship, so do allow yourself that emotion. Do things that make you happy, for example, volunteer to help others; socialize with friends; or rediscover favourite hobbies. Be bold and brave and believe in yourself – you can achieve what you want and build an exciting future. All these things will help you boost your self-esteem, so embrace your freedom and the positive emotions and energy it brings.

19

# Revamp Your Image

When you're stuck in a rut, sometimes you need to take drastic action. An image revamp is a fun way to inject some vitality back into your life.

'A change is as good as a rest', so the saying goes. Perhaps you need a confidence boost after the end of a relationship or you're about to start a new job. Whatever the reason for your reinvention, it should never be to keep other people happy – do it just for you. Feel empowered and enjoy the fact that you have the ability to take control and blast your way out of that rut.

### GOALS

- Release a blast of new-found energy.
- Be brave, be bold and enjoy embracing change.
- Find a new you who's ready grab the world with two hands and give it a good shake!

## DECLUTTER YOUR WARDROBE

Be ruthless. Start by taking everything out – the idea is to only put back what you want to keep. Have you worn the item in the last year? If not, ditch it. Despite any possible scenarios you conjure up, it's highly unlikely it will get worn. Do you like it? Don't keep something because it's the height of fashion and you're 'supposed' to like it – only keep what you enjoy wearing. Now you've made some space, think about what items the 'new you' needs. Book yourself a personal stylist session at a department store, tell them what you're aiming for and they'll help you find looks that work and create a wardrobe that's unique to you. Alternatively, take a trusted friend shopping with you – it's a great way to get encouragement to buy things you'd normally shy away from.

## HAIR'S TO A NEW YOU!

Our hairstyle is integral to our identity. When we find a style we like, we're prone to cling on to it. A new look for your hair makes a huge impact, but it's a big step if you're thinking of something drastic, so follow these tips for getting it right:

- Find a stylist you trust and who shares your vision. Your usual person may be fantastic for maintenance cuts, but do you trust them to give you a whole new look? Recommendations from other people are the way forward.

- Take photos of the styles you like along to your appointment. But don't get too attached to one style – if the stylist tells you it won't suit you or that it won't work with your hair, listen to them!

- Can you handle your new hairstyle? If you're prone to oversleep and have to rush to work in 5 minutes flat, don't choose a high maintenance style that requires an hour in front of the mirror. Think big but think practical!

## FACE UP TO IT

Whether you like a lot of makeup or prefer the bare minimum, it's time to revamp your makeup bag to complement your new hair and wardrobe. We're all guilty of letting makeup products fester in drawers so have a good clear out of the ones you no longer use and start afresh. An in-store appointment is a great way to get a mini-makeover and find recommendations for products that suit you and accentuate your best bits. Be firm about what you like so you don't emerge looking like a clown on a drunken night out.

# Kickstart an Exercise Regime

This is a sure-fire way to see and feel rapid change in your life. So pull on some joggers and feed your body and soul.

Write a list of the benefits of exercise and you'll find it's a long one. What's more, it's full of no-brainer reasons for getting off your couch – most of which will change your life from Day 1. If you're not exercising, what's your excuse? Not enough time? Don't enjoy it? Fear of being surrounded by lithe types in Lycra? Forget the lame excuses, it's time to reclaim exercise for YOU.

## GOALS

- Set realistic goals for what you want to achieve.
- Change your mindset so that exercise becomes a normal part of your routine.
- Embrace the health-boosting benefits and live a longer life!

## SET YOUR GOALS

Before you even buy new trainers, write a list of what you want to get out of exercise. Is it to tone up? Lose weight? Improve your stamina? Get your mental well-being back on track? Give your heart a workout? De-stress and relax? The results you want may determine the type of exercise you do. Be realistic about timescales. You'll immediately feel the benefits of post-exercise feel-good chemicals rushing through you but achieving your goals should be long-term. Be patient and you'll soon see the results you want.

## BUILDING FITNESS INTO YOUR LIFE

Don't have the time for exercise? Simple answer: make time. Your physical and mental well-being are worth the effort. Upping your daily activity will quickly show benefits and it doesn't have to be a full-on gym session. Simple things you can do NOW include:

- Take the stairs rather than the elevator.
- Get off one train/bus stop earlier and walk the rest of the way.
- Call a friend and plan a hike/cycle/countryside walk rather than your usual night out in a bar.
- Walk, don't take the car. (A bonus if you fancy a glass of something ...)
- Book a free introductory session at your local gym (most offer free passes).

Starting small is a great way to boost your confidence, kickstart the fitness bug and make healthy living a big part of your life.

## FIND SOMETHING YOU ENJOY

If you don't look forward to exercise, you'll never stick at it. Try out lots of different things – including outside your comfort zone! – until you find something that clicks. You may have snubbed yoga only to discover you're a Downward-Facing Dog addict. So, get down to your local sports centre and find out what classes and clubs they offer. Find out what your friends enjoy and tag along. Be bold, be brave and don't be embarrassed to find out you're useless at something – just try something else!

## STAY MOTIVATED

With anything new and exciting, the challenge is to sustain that energy beyond the first 24 hours. Sitting down and planning your long-term goals is an important starting point. If you find yourself getting bored with an activity, shake it up a bit – do a different activity (and use different muscles!) and then come back to it.

Try to set aside a regular time for exercise so that you get into the habit and it becomes part of your routine. Exercising with other people is also an effective way to get you up and at it – there's nothing like a persistent friend dragging you out of bed at six in the morning!

27

# Quit Smoking

Smell like an ashtray?
Tired of coughing?
Want to live longer?
It's time to stub out
your last cigarette
and quit the habit.

Completely quitting smoking takes longer than 24 hours. This is about getting yourself in the right mindset to kickstart it. Without facing the cold, hard reality of why you choose to smoke and the implications it has, you can't make that decision to quit. You need to be 100% behind the process for it to be a success.

**GOALS (THERE'S JUST ONE)**
- At the risk of stating the obvious: save your life and save your money!

## WHY DO YOU SMOKE?

Identify what's got you into the habit of smoking. Is it peer pressure? Something you've just always done? Think it looks cool? Ask yourself whether these are genuine reasons for continuing to smoke. Once you accept there's no real rationale for doing it, you've given yourself the impetus to quit.

## MAKE A PLAN

Make a list of all the positive reasons for quitting. Put it somewhere you'll see it constantly, for example, on your refrigerator or in your wallet/purse. The reasons could include:

- Feeling better and healthier and being able to run for a bus without wheezing.
- Smelling sweeter!
- Extending your life and the lives of those around you who'll no longer be inhaling your second-hand smoke.
- Saving money – not just small change, but A LOT.

If you need a short, sharp shock to remind yourself why you're quitting, keep a photo of a loved one to hand. One look at that and you'll rapidly get your motivation back.

## THINK POSITIVE

Don't *hope* you can stop – *believe* you can! Congratulate yourself on small victories. Even one smoke-free day is a massive step in the right direction and proves you can do it. Try to visualise yourself in 5 years' time as a non-smoker – consider all the ways your life will have improved, in particular the quality and length of your life. Don't beat yourself up about minor slip-ups. Rather than be discouraged, simply get back on the wagon and learn from whatever weakness prompted you to fall off it.

## BEAT THE CRAVING

Nicotine cravings can last for up to 5 minutes. Your challenge is to get through and out the other side. Being prepared will help you crack it:

- Distract yourself until the craving passes – leave the room and do something else; if you're at a party, get up and dance; call a friend; tackle a Rubik's Cube!
- Nicotine replacement therapy, e.g. over-the-counter patches or gum – these can help you overcome intense cravings.
- Avoid situations where you're most likely to have a cigarette, e.g. coffee breaks with colleagues, boozy nights out – at least until you're able to handle them.
- Work on relaxation techniques to keep your stress levels low. Stress itself may trigger your smoking and quitting will be a stressful time.
- Don't be tempted to have 'just one'! It's likely to lead to another …

Finally, have you worked out how much smoking is costing you? Guaranteed, it will be quite a shock. Plan what you can put the money towards instead and start saving it – perhaps a holiday, your favourite band's big summer gig, or a new car. Give yourself a reward to aim for and you'll have a big incentive to stay on the straight and narrow. Good luck – quitting smoking is hard, but you can do it.

# Spring Clean Your Social Media

Do you *really* have 3,500 'friends'?!? Time to start living in the real world.

Social networking takes up an inordinate amount of time, sucks us into a vortex and then spits us out glassy-eyed. If the amount of information appearing in your timeline is so vast that you miss what the people you *really* care about are saying, it's time to start clicking the 'unfriend' or 'follow' button. Reducing the stream of information that the digital age bombards you with can only bring your stress levels down. And thanks to the immediacy of social media, the effect is instant!

**GOALS**

- Declutter your social media – ditch the 'noise' and focus on *real* friends.
- Reduce the time you spend trawling through meaningless drivel feeling bad about yourself.
- Increase the time you have for living in the real world!

**START WITH THE QUICK FIXES**

The short, sharp cull approach may feel a bit harsh but if you want to make big changes, you need to put yourself first. Here's how to get started:

- Unfollow anyone who doesn't follow you.

- Unfollow anyone who irritates you or makes your heart sink. It could be because they bombard you with cat videos or perhaps they hold unsavoury political views.

- Switch off your notifications. A barrage of alerts that has you constantly reaching for your phone is a horrible drain on your time.

- If you're really worried about upsetting someone on social media, just hide their updates from your timeline rather than 'defriend' or 'unfollow' them.

- Unfollow those retailers who are forever luring you in with sales and sucking cash out of you.

## KEEP IT MANAGEABLE

Fantastic – you're through the initial spring clean. Hopefully you're feeling wonderfully liberated. Now it's time to keep up the hard work and become a *discerning* social media user. It's all too easy to become overwhelmed again so think twice before you add anyone new to your networks. Like with Marie Kondo's decluttering mantra, ask yourself whether they bring joy to your life – if they don't, then don't connect with them. Simple. Your social network should be positive and supportive so think about what *you* need, rather than making other people happy.

## SOCIAL MEDIA AND WELL-BEING

"Why go to all this effort?" I hear you ask. It's not an effort – spring cleaning your social media is quick and reaps fast results. Clearing time and headspace is vitally important for your mental and emotional well-being – something not to be underestimated. Social media is brilliant in many ways but can also wield a negative influence that sees you compare yourself to other people's lives (filtered) and bodies (yes, filtered). Dissatisfaction, low self-esteem and a poor body image can all be by-products of social media. Eliminate negative influences from your life and you'll feel a weight lift off your shoulders.

# Have a Digital Detox

If you recorded how much time you spend on electronic devices each day, you'd be shocked. Try ditching digital for 24 hours and see what happens. **Hint:** it's great.

With smartphones and the internet taking over the world, our digital well-being is a hot topic. Technology has a huge part to play in our lives, but we need to make sure we strike the right balance. Are you missing out on things in the real world because you're glued to a virtual world? Are you feeling the pressure to look and live a certain way? Being dragged into constantly checking our devices steals so much valuable time.

### GOALS
- Switch off all your digital devices for 24 hours.
- Reconnect with the real world.
- Use the time wasted online to rediscover the things you love.

### HOW DETOX IS THE DETOX?

To get the most out of a digital detox in a short space of time, you need to throw yourself into it 100%. No "I'll just have a quick check …" and definitely no hiding in the bathroom to update Instagram. You need to go digital cold turkey. For just one day, your challenge is to not check social media, switch off your mobile, unplug your tablet or PC, and even leave your TV switched off. This isn't about going back to the Dark Ages, it's about giving yourself a chance to rediscover a life not glued to a screen. Remember that once upon a time, people existed without the internet. Guess what? They survived!

## REAP THE OFFLINE REWARDS

You might find it hard to believe that a 24-hour digital detox could change your life, but it can. Rediscover your perspective on life and channel your time in a more positive way:

- Your productivity levels will rocket. Taking a break from technology will show just how much time you waste on it.

- Reboot your social connections. If you're constantly attached to the internet, your connections in the real world have probably taken a back seat. Use your detox time to meet friends and family you've not seen for a while.

- When you look away from a screen you immediately start to appreciate the turning of the world. Live in the present and don't let the good things around you pass you by. Without devices buzzing at you for your attention, you'll feel much less stressed.

- If you're always online, people will expect to get a response from you 24/7. Redress the balance and be available on YOUR terms. Respond at a time that's convenient for you.

• Use the time you free up to invest in the things you love. Rediscover your neglected passions – reading, drawing, walking – and feel your sense of fulfilment grow.

**KEEPING IT GOING**

Getting your digital usage at a level that doesn't affect your well-being is about striking a balance. The occasional 24 hours offline will do you wonders, but of course in reality it's impossible to switch off completely all the time. Instead, think about how you can reduce your screen time and start building good habits. Switch off notification sounds so that you're not constantly distracted. Resist the urge to continuously check your email and social media – set aside short chunks of time each day for reviewing, responding and posting. Don't feel compelled to reply to everything within one minute of it arriving in your inbox.

39

# Meet the Love of Your Life

With endless distractions and hectic lives, meeting 'the one' is becoming harder and harder in the modern world.

Constantly staying late at work? Addicted to social media and your emails rather than looking up at your surroundings? Have a limited cashflow so you can't go out as much? These are just some of the reasons why it seems harder to meet your soulmate in today's world.

## GOALS

- Stop thinking that good things only happen to other people – take the initiative and make good things happen to you!
- Get yourself out there and stop hiding your light behind a bushel.
- Know your own mind – what do you want from love?

## GIVE YOURSELF A BREAK

To find love, you first need to work on loving yourself. This can be incredibly tough if you're not used to being kind to yourself, but start to retrain your mind and you can undo those bad habits. Try these for a kickstart:

- Counter negative self-criticism with a positive statement. "Look at my belly!" becomes "My body is amazing – it's strong and beautiful."

- Acknowledge that no one's perfect and stop pretending to be someone you're not. Embrace EVERY quirky, weird, funny, loving and passionate part of you – it's what makes you, YOU. Be proud of it.

## PLAN IT OUT

Too often we spend time waiting for things to happen to us. If you believe that love will happen when you least expect it, you might just find yourself waiting a *very* long time! You need to help make it happen. Write up a list of the type of person you would like to meet and what you think you should get out of love. It may sound a little clinical, but life's too short to be wasting your time constantly dating the wrong people. By creating some focus, you can channel your efforts and the fact that you're doing something will provide a wonderful injection of positivity.

## SPEED DATING

If you're time poor, try speed dating. This quick way to meet a lot of different people in one evening is making a comeback. It's a scattergun approach of course – you'll meet people you'd not to want to see again in a million years but that's pretty much life, just compressed into a couple of hours! Try these top tips for getting a top date:

- Don't talk about work, religion or politics. Find out what they enjoy/what their hobbies are– it's far more illuminating.
- Talk but also LISTEN – the key to a strong relationship.
- Pre-plan some great questions: What 3 items couldn't you live without? How do you like to spend a Sunday?

## SIGN UP TO AN INTERNET DATING SITE

Disillusioned with swiping left on apps to find yourself a quick date? Go retro and sign yourself up to a good old-fashioned dating website. Make sure you do your research first. Which one are you most likely to find like-minded people on? Is there a site that better suits your own outlook on love?

Register online and then craft your profile. Use photos that reflect your interests and personality rather than just your looks. Include some conversation starters that will prompt a question. Don't be negative – make sure you sound like a happy and positive person and you'll attract similar people. Try to show what you're like rather than tell people – for example, if you're funny, add something humorous to your profile rather than just describe yourself as having a GSOH.

If you're struggling to think of what to put on your profile, ask a friend for some advice or to write it for you. Remember to check what they've written before you post it!

# Make Your Peace with Someone

It's easy to fall out with someone. It can be over something major or something you can't even remember. If you want to make amends – do it.

Relationships with family and friends aren't always rosy. Tensions can arise in all kinds of situations – births, marriages, deaths, nights out, wrong looks, misinterpreted comments – the list is endless. Whatever has happened to cause a relationship to sour, it will of course take time to rebuild the connection you had. However, in less than 24 hours you can take those important first steps to repair the relationship. Prepare yourself, then pick up the phone or write an email/letter.

## GOALS

- Accept responsibility and make amends.
- Say sorry with sincerity – and spell out what you're sorry for.
- Forgive yourself and the other person.

## SWALLOW YOUR PRIDE

Things can seem hard to undo, especially if they've gone on for a long time. If you're thinking about making peace with someone, it's likely that a switch may already have flicked in your mind and you're prepared to swallow your pride. Mistakes are hard to digest, but by admitting you're wrong and exposing a weakness, you're showing how strong you are:

- The constructive admission, "I've made a mistake, but I know how to fix it right away".
- The humble admission, "I got that completely wrong, I took my eye off the ball".
- The promise-to-do-better admission, "I really messed that up. It won't happen again".

## SAY SORRY

No one likes to apologise – it won't be easy. If you're not sincere, you might as well not bother. A good apology means laying yourself bare. It shouldn't be self-centred (focus on what you're apologising for, not on how you feel), incomplete (accepts responsibility but doesn't touch on regret or redemption) or argumentative ("I'm sorry, but ..."). Accept responsibility for what's happened and properly and directly apologise for what you've done and the impact it had.

Remember, forgiveness isn't automatic – it's up to the other person to accept your apology so don't give up immediately if you're snubbed.

## MAKING AMENDS

Redeeming yourself needs to be part of making peace. Think of what you can do to fix what has happened or how to stop it happening again. If you've bad-mouthed someone, speak to whoever you misinformed and put the record straight. If you broke something, replace it. If your bad behaviour was the root of the problem, find ways to improve it (e.g. anger management classes). Seeking redemption is the best way to make your apology sincere.

## FORGIVENESS

Gandhi once said that "Forgiveness is the attribute of the strong". He's spot on – forgiving can be harder than apologising and to do it shows real strength of character. It might not be immediate, but it can come with time so be patient with the person you're apologising to. They may need time to process your apology and accept its sincerity so give them that space once you've made the first steps towards peace. Equally, if you're feeling bad about your actions, you need to forgive yourself. We all make mistakes. Acknowledge what you can learn from the experience, resolve to not let it happen in future and – most of all – be kind to yourself.

# Plan a Family

Not a random conversation for a Saturday night, but something to do with your partner or spouse when you both feel the time is right. The implications are certainly life-changing!

There are lots of factors to consider when you're thinking about starting a family. And there's no doubt that it's a BIG conversation. Even if you and your partner agree, there is still a lot to discuss before you hit the bedroom.

**GOALS**
- Have an honest and open conversation with your partner about starting a family.
- Answer the big question: are you ready?
- Get practical about the impact on your lives.

## ARE YOU READY TO HAVE CHILDREN?

Keen to start straight away? Curb your enthusiasm and consider the pros and cons. It's an amazing life-changing experience but also a daunting responsibility. Points to consider:

- Where are you in your jobs/careers? Is now a good time to take a break or is there something else you want to achieve? Little people do have the habit of curtailing your time. So, if your upcoming dream promotion means travelling the world for six months a year, perhaps postpone starting a family.

- Having children doesn't mean your life must stop. However, is there anything on your bucket list that you'd like to do first? Perhaps you want to spend a year roughing it through Asia or volunteer for a charity overseas. Get these ticked off before taking on family responsibilities.

- Can you imagine a life where you can't do exactly what you want, when you want?! This is the reality of having responsibility for children. If you can't imagine being selfless, is being a parent really for you?

## CAN YOU AFFORD IT?

According to research, the cost of raising a child to the age of 18 for a couple in the UK is £75,436 – include childcare costs and that rises to £155,100! The outlay for getting your home ready for a baby is also substantial. Whilst some items you can borrow, inherit or buy second-hand, there are many you'll need to buy new. And if you can't borrow or buy second-hand, there are expensive essentials that you simply can't do without (e.g. pram/buggy, cot, baby monitor and bottles/sterilisers).

BUT if you *do* want a family, don't let this put you off. Just be aware of the financial impact of supporting a tiny human being and plan your budget carefully (see the chapter on Create a Budget, page 52).

## THE PRACTICALITIES

It's easy to overlook the practicalities when you're going 'goo-goo ga-ga' over the prospect of the pitter-patter of tiny feet. Keep one foot in the realm of reality if you can.

• Start by thinking about your car. Is it suitable for a carrying a child and all the associated paraphernalia? This generally means ditching your two-seater sports car for something with five seats and a cavernous trunk.

• Is your home big enough? Do you have enough room to start a family? If not, then what are the costs of moving?

• What about childcare? Will you or your partner leave work to take on the role of full-time carer? Or switch to part-time work? If you're planning alternative childcare options, what would they be and how much would they cost?

If that all makes sense and you're good to go, then have fun doing it! In 24 hours' time, things might be very different and you won't even know it yet …

# Create a Budget

It may sound dull but creating a budget is a great (and sensible) way to plan for something you want and get your finances in order!

There are lots of benefits to having control of your finances. For starters, knowing you're not living beyond your means reduces stress and uncertainty. If your money is in a muddle, the prospect of addressing it can seem a daunting one. But take a deep breath and you'll discover it's quick and easy and makes a big difference. You don't even need to be a numbers guru or a whizz with spreadsheets.

## GOALS

- Get to grips with how much you're spending versus your income.
- Set in place plans to reduce your debts.
- Start to save for a dream.

### KNOW WHERE YOUR MONEY GOES

Grab a pen and paper or grab your laptop and open Excel. However you do it, you need to start by writing down what you're spending and the bills going out of your bank account (outgoings) versus the money coming in. Itemise everything – not only for precision but also to highlight those areas you could be cutting down or eliminating entirely. Once everything is noted, you'll be able to see how much spare cash you do (or don't!) have left at the end of the month. This is where you can start to take control.

## WHAT'S LEFT IN THE COFFERS?

If you're lucky enough to have money spare, you can start to put it towards life-changing uses:

- Start paying off debts. No matter the size, chipping away at debts is a great step forward (see below).

- Save! Save! Save! Have you always wanted to retrain for your perfect job? Is there somewhere in the world you've dreamed of visiting since you were a child? Perhaps money has so far prevented you from doing these things. If you start saving towards a goal, it's an amazing way to change the direction of your life. Even saving a tiny amount towards a dream will fill you with positive vibes.

## DEBT BUSTING

Debts are incredibly draining, putting pressure on you mentally as well as stopping you from being able to spend money on things you love. If you can set aside money to pay off debts, start with the high-interest debts – if you're a homeowner this will be your mortgage. Getting rid of the most expensive debts will free up the most money. No, you can't pay off your mortgage in 24 hours but you can set in place a plan now that will benefit you hugely in the future.

## QUICK STARTS TO SAVING MONEY

- Paying too much for your car, home insurance or utilities? Make use of online comparison sites and switch providers if you find a better deal.

- Simple things like switching off lights, not leaving your TV on standby and avoiding running taps unnecessarily will save money on energy and utility bills.

- Get busy on online selling sites and sell all those items you don't want/need anymore.

- Buy cheaper brand alternatives when doing your weekly food shop.

- Ditch those monthly subscriptions that you've let run because you're too lazy to cancel them!

# Buy a New Home

So you can't *actually* buy a property in 24 hours, but you can decide what and where and decipher the puzzling process that is home buying.

Buying a home is a bewildering process, especially if it's your first time. It can be long and stressful with many ups and downs. If you're serious about making this big change in your life, you can't achieve it in a day, but what you can do is sit down and plan thoroughly. Narrow down your options based on lifestyle, location and affordability. Also think about the future and what you might need if circumstances change, for example, space for children or to work from home.

**GOALS**
- Get a clear idea of what you want.
- Figure out your finances and what you can afford.
- Master the house buying process so that it doesn't master you!

## WHAT ARE YOU LOOKING FOR?

Do you want a house or an apartment? Detached? A big garden? Two bathrooms? Modern or traditional? Get all your 'wants' down on paper. There will be A LOT so the next step is to prioritise. What features are your 'must-haves' and what are just 'nice-to-have'? This will help you narrow down your search and – if lots of properties meet your criteria – decide between the options. This process will also help prevent arguments if you're buying with someone – make sure you agree on what you want!

## WHERE DO YOU WANT TO LIVE?

As the saying goes, 'location, location, location'. You might want to be close to family or it might be more important to be near work. Are there good transport links? Is there a great school nearby and somewhere to go when you run out of milk at midnight? Again, this will help narrow down your search and make you *really* think about what you want. There are always going to be compromises, so as with the property features, consider which location specifics you're willing to give up in order to find the right property.

## CAN YOU AFFORD IT?

The BIG question. There's no point in house-hunting without knowing what you can afford. Work out how much the monthly cost of owning a home would be (including mortgage, insurance, taxes, bills) and compare it to your current income. Do you have the money for a down payment/ deposit? If not, it might be better to take time to save rather than borrow it. Speak to your bank and go online to look at the mortgage deals on offer that suit your needs. Don't feel pressured to keep up with the Joneses and overstretch yourself – it might mean compromises but at least you won't be left in crippling debt.

## KNOW YOUR ENEMY

If you understand the house buying rules inside and out, you're more likely to avoid problems. Get your head around the process – what do you need to prepare in advance and what needs to happen when? Speak to friends and family who've recently purchased or get online to find useful advice. Having a handle on the jargon can stop you being flummoxed by lawyers and realtors/agents. With regard to the latter, make sure you use a good one. The best ones won't try to sell you something way out of your price range, they'll keep in contact with regular updates and they'll get you into properties before they're marketed.

# Declutter Your House

You might not be able to do this in 24 hours. However, by making quick in-roads into decluttering you can start to turn your living space around.

Humans can't help but accumulate clutter. There are many reasons for this: pressure on us as consumers to buy goods; a desire to stockpile for the future; hanging onto gifts we'd feel guilty if we gave away; an instinct to collect; and an emotional attachment to objects. But clutter can have a negative effect on our well-being. If the clutter in your house is overwhelming and making you stressed, taking the practical steps to declutter will restore a sense of calm and boost your energy levels.

## GOALS

- Get the decluttering bug and, one room at a time, pave the way for a more organised, harmonious home and life.
- Reap the emotional benefits of going clutter-free (less stress, a greater sense of clarity and a more contented mind).

### GET STARTED

Decide what your realistic decluttering goals are. Do you want to tackle the most cluttered room that will make the biggest difference to your life? Or tick off the smaller challenges first? If your goals are too ambitious you may find yourself overwhelmed before you even get started, so break down the bigger jobs into smaller tasks. Make sure you're working to a realistic timeline – if you're easily distracted you may find that decluttering takes longer than expected. As big as the task may seem, try and visualise yourself living free of clutter, with a greater sense of well-being and with more time to enjoy the things you love.

**THE FOUR-BOX CHALLENGE**

Now you're ready to get going, grab four boxes:

• Box one should contain items that you will donate to charity or to friends/family.

• For box two, add the things that don't need to be on display and can be stored away.

• Box three is for the items that can be sold.

• Add anything that can be thrown away or recycled into box four.

Each box has a specific purpose designed to focus your mind and organize the decluttering process.

**HELP! I WANT TO KEEP EVERYTHING**

It's tough but you can do it! For each item you pick up, ask yourself:

• Do I use this?

- Do I have more than one of these?
- Would I buy it again?
- Does it really make my life easier?
- Do I love it?

Your answers will decide whether the item is for keeping, donating, storing elsewhere or throwing away/recycling. And one final question: does it belong here? If something shouldn't even be in that room, it needs to be guided back to its appropriate home. You've got to grab decluttering by the horns. Be brutal and decisive!

## KEEP CONTROL OF THE CLUTTER

Decluttering creates a new, potentially life-changing mindset to move forward with. As much as you want to maintain the results, you may find yourself slipping back into old, untidy ways. Just regroup and retackle. On top of your usual housework, take 10 minutes once a week in each room and have a quick tidy-up of anything pushing your clutter boundaries. Little and often is the best way forward. When you're considering buying something new, ask yourself if you *really* need it. Will it just create clutter? If you find it hard to resist, put in place a 'one in, one out' rule: if you buy something, you need to remove something else.

# Overcome a Fear

Fear can be absolutely crippling and stop you living your life as fully as you want to. It's time to take a deep breath and face your demons ...

Fear is one of our most natural responses and has kept us alive in the face of danger for millennia. However, in the modern world it's an instinct that isn't always helpful. When fear affects your life, the things you do and the choices you make, it can be debilitating. Fear and anxiety might feel like bad feelings you can't shake – but you can. It won't happen overnight but recognising something needs to change NOW is a huge step in the right direction.

## GOALS

- Plan strategies for dealing with fear when it strikes.
- Push yourself outside your comfort zone to conquer your fear.
- Learn to analyse your thoughts and how they're tricking you.

## BE PREPARED

Arm yourself with ways to deal with feelings of fear as soon as they mount. If you can prevent the feelings and physical symptoms escalating into something more overwhelming, you'll be better able to take control. Write a plan of things you

can do to calm yourself and take the edge off the fear,
for example:

- A relaxing breathing technique that works for you (not all will
  so experiment).
- A happy place you can visualise yourself in.
- Discover the pressure points on your hands that are calming
  when massaged.
- What might help distract you? Playing a game on your
  phone; counting five things around you that you see/hear/
  touch/smell/taste; reading a book; looking at photos of
  loved ones.

### ANALYSE YOUR THOUGHT PROCESS

Challenging your thought process and those troublesome
"what ifs?" can rid fear of its power over you. You don't need
to wait until you're actually feeling fearful to do this. Think
about the thoughts that go through your head when you're in
a situation that scares you. It might be "I'm going to embarrass
myself"; it could even be "I'm going to have a heart attack and
die". Now, think about the likelihood of these things actually
happening. Can you make yourself have a heart attack if you're
breathing fast? No.

When those unhelpful thoughts go through your mind, just let them pass. Don't dwell on them, simply let them drift away safe in the knowledge that they are only thoughts and that you have control of them – not vice versa.

## DON'T AVOID YOUR FEAR

Avoidance of your fear will only enlarge it. You've no doubt heard the phrase "feel the fear and do it anyway" – so confront your fear head on. For example, if you hate using the elevator, do it anyway, don't take the stairs. This will teach your brain through experience that in reality nothing terrible is going to happen. It's hard work (and stressful) but if you can retrain your brain out of the bad habits that automatically trigger feelings of fear in certain situations, you will disarm the fear itself.

## TALK TO SOMEONE

There's no embarrassment in having a fear or phobia. But if it's disrupting your life and your own strategies for dealing with it aren't working, TALK TO SOMEONE. Sometimes just saying things out loud to another person can help you rationalise your fears and see them for what they are. A friend might offer to accompany you into a situation you find stressful and help you breathe your way through it. Make use of that support.

# Reboot Your Diet

It's easy to be lazy about eating well. Time, convenience and cooking skills can all contribute towards a poor (and often expensive) diet.

This doesn't mean switching to only organic food or to cook everything from scratch, but there are plenty of small changes you can make that will have a big impact. And of course, it takes no longer than 24 hours to reboot your diet and get back on track.

## GOALS

- Eat more healthily and tip the balance between the rubbish in your fridge and the good stuff.
- Replace your bad habits with good habits.
- Rediscover (or discover for the first time!) cooking.

### BLITZ THAT KITCHEN

If you're serious about change, you need to blitz your cupboards. No one's saying you shouldn't have treats or eat the naughty foods you love, but moderation is key. If that packet of sweets is there for when you get back from work late and can't be bothered to eat properly, donate them to a friend or the office to eliminate the temptation. Get rid of anything that's out of date or that you know you're never going to eat.

### GET DOWN TO THE GROCERY STORE

Cooking your own meals doesn't need to be fancy so get the staples for a healthy, balanced diet – fish, meat, eggs, olive oil, cheese, brown rice and pasta, fresh fruit and vegetables. Get the basic dried herbs and spices that'll give a *zing* to any meal – Italian seasoning, parsley, curry powder, cumin, paprika. Pick up a supply of healthy snacks – try nuts, olives, natural yoghurt, fruit – that will stop you reaching for the sugary treats.

### BUY A COOKERY BOOK

Start off with something that promises simplicity, speed and minimal ingredients. Cooking for yourself will help you avoid ready meals, which tend to be packed with sugar and fat. Have fun – this could be a life-changing passion you're about to discover!

### BREAKFAST BOOST

Are your cereals packed with sugar? All they're giving you is a quick energy fix that will barely last until lunchtime. Avoid the crash and get some eggs on your plate. Combine with fruit or veg and you'll find your energy boosted big time (and you're less likely to crave a mid-morning snack).

### IN WITH THE GOOD, OUT WITH THE BAD

Sugar and refined carbohydrates are some of the unhealthiest parts of modern diets. Wave goodbye to low nutrient and low fibre food. Try ditching the simple carbs (refined bread, white rice and pasta, sweets, sugary drinks, etc.) and switch in the good stuff (unrefined bread, wholegrains, bran cereals, legumes, fresh fruit and veg).

## EMOTIONAL EATING

Everyone has rubbish days when all you want to do is eat a massive slab of chocolate. When you reach for a snack, ask yourself "why?". If you're not actually hungry then step away. Put on your favourite music and dance around your living room instead – it's a far healthier way to get the same feel-good boost.

## START CHECKING LABELS

Know how to decipher labels so you can make low-saturated fat, low-salt, low-sugar choices:

- Total fat: High – more than 17.5g of fat per 100g. Low – 3g or less per 100g.

- Saturated fat: High – more than 5g per 100g. Low – 1.5g or less per 100g.

- Sugars: High – more than 22.5g per 100g. Low – 5g or less per 100g.

- Salt: High – more than 1.5g per 100g (or 0.6g sodium). Low – 0.3g or less per 100g (or 0.1g sodium).

# Give a Little, Gain a Lot

Helping other people or a good cause is incredibly rewarding. Volunteer your time and see first-hand how you can change lives – and change yours.

There are so many big global issues affecting our world – climate change, wars, plastic in our oceans – that we often feel powerless to make a difference. But whilst it's governments and corporations who need to make the big changes, individuals making small changes can have an impact too.

**GOALS**

- Identify local causes you're passionate about and volunteer your time and skills.
- Learn new skills and meet new people that could send your life in an unexpected direction.
- Re-evaluate your priorities in life and discover what is important to you.

## THINK LOCAL

If you're looking for somewhere to volunteer your time – start local. It could be a homeless shelter, a food bank, a community centre, or an animal shelter. Get in touch with organisations who specifically co-ordinate volunteers for community groups and charities. Volunteers aren't always easy to come by so any charities needing help will definitely be asking for it! Alternatively, make a list of local charities that represent a cause you feel passionate about and call or email them. It's guaranteed that within 24 hours you'll have someone accepting your offer of help. Even if you start off just handing out leaflets at an event, your contribution will be valued hugely.

## THE POSITIVE BENEFITS OF VOLUNTEERING

Whilst you might be volunteering primarily to make a difference, it can also help achieve personal goals or overcome obstacles you've struggled with. Perhaps you've been through a tough time and need to rebuild your self-esteem. If you're feeling lonely, volunteering is a great way to get out there and meet like-minded people. Giving something back benefits everyone:

- Grow your confidence. Trying something new builds a real sense of achievement.
- Make a difference. See first-hand the positive effect you can have on the lives of people and communities.
- Meet people, make new friends and feel part of a community.
- Learn new skills and gain experience – all great for your CV!

## WHO KNOWS WHAT IT WILL SPARK!

Volunteering gives you the chance to roll your sleeves up and pitch in with all kinds of activities. You'll discover skills you never knew you had and things you're brilliant at. It's a great opportunity to explore what you're capable of. You might find ideas for a whole new career emerging. Simply meeting someone inspirational could send your life off in a whole new direction.

Your sense of perspective will also change. What's felt important to you before will take on new meaning when you're exposed to other people's experiences. You may find that you re-evaluate your own life as a result. Giving something back to the community – and as a result the wider world – can be truly life-changing.

# Plan a Dream Trip

Is there somewhere you've always dreamed of visiting? Dust off that case and passport. Plan ahead now and that dream shall be yours.

Never accept a dream is just a dream. Dither and procrastinate and you might just find the opportunity has passed. If you have a dream trip, it's time to make it a reality. Challenge yourself to finally sit down and plan it out. You're not only planning a life-changing experience, the excitement and anticipation will be incredibly special too.

## GOALS
- Plan, plan, plan! Make your biggest dream into a life-changing reality.
- Overcome the fears that are stopping you.
- Get set for a horizon-expanding adventure!

### PLAN AHEAD

Throwing caution to the wind might seem like the spirit of adventure, but planning is key to making your trip successful. Even if it's a dream you've been mulling over for years, start by asking yourself some questions: "Where?" "What?" "When?" "How much?" And make sure you can answer "Why?" With the answers clear in your mind, get researching. With the internet at your fingertips there's no excuse for not discovering all the ins and outs that'll make your trip amazing. Plus, it's the perfect

77

place to compare prices for flights and accommodation and get the best deals.

## OVERCOME YOUR FEARS

If fear of the unknown has stopped you planning your dream trip, don't worry – you're perfectly normal! You could be feeling fearful for several reasons: perhaps you're afraid of travelling alone; you're worried about safety; or you're worried that the reality won't live up to the dream. It's likely you're imagining obstacles that aren't there. Assess how real the risks are on a scale of 1–10. Pre-think any likely risks in a rational way and how you can work around or limit them. No one said a life-changing adventure has to be boring, but it's not about recklessness!

## THE BORING MONEY BIT

Inevitably, finances are a consideration when planning a dream trip. Even if you're not going to travel far, you still need money to do it. Do be realistic and avoid getting yourself in debt, but don't let money stop you from following your dream. Save like a demon if you need to – that's all part of the adventure. You'll need to create a budget to decide how much you can realistically save and set out the likely costs of your trip. Could you make money from your trip? Perhaps by working along the way (if it's a long trip) or by writing about it when you get back. Could you take a work sabbatical, giving you the security of a salary to return to?

## REAP THE REWARDS

Besides the amazing feeling of having achieved a dream, don't underestimate the life-changing benefits your experience will bring:

- The chance to step back from the everyday and gain a fresh perspective on life.
- Conquer your fears.
- Beat stress.
- Learn how to handle new and unexpected situations.
- Discover how flexible and adaptable you can be.
- Improve your self-confidence.

Travel can have a wonderfully positive impact on all aspects of your life, so grasp that dream!

# Change Your Sleep Habits

We underestimate the impact lack of sleep has on our physical and mental well-being. If you're sleep starved, the good news is you can make a change ... tonight.

We've all been there. Staring impatiently at the clock, huffing and puffing as the time drifts by. The mind more alert than it's ever been, even though it could barely function all day. Life doesn't have to be sleepless and counting sheep isn't the only way to fix it.

### GOALS
- Find the optimum number of hours you need to wake up full of energy.
- Devise strategies to get you off the sofa and into bed early.
- Create a sleep-friendly environment.

## HOW MUCH SLEEP?

Some people can function on as little as six hours of sleep. Others need 10 hours! However, most adults need seven to nine hours sleep a night. Aim for seven hours to start with – if you feel tired during the day or struggle to get out of bed then make your bedtime 15 minutes earlier. Repeat this until your body tells you it's getting enough rest. How do you know? You'll be ready to get up when your alarm goes off, you'll not get tired during the day (less head-swallowing yawns) and you'll be less likely to crave carbs and sugar.

### THE BENEFITS

Changing your sleep habits brings an immediate benefit. If you don't feel better after your first night of extra sleep, keep up the hard work and in just two to three days you'll start feeling like a new person. Getting enough sleep has a long list of benefits as it:

• Reduces stress and lifts your mood.

• Helps to improve memory and concentration.

• Lowers blood pressure and the risk of heart disease/strokes.

• Enables you to maintain your weight.

• Boosts daytime energy levels.

• Improves exercise performance.

• Allows for a more effective and productive brain.

• Enables you to deal with day-to-day life better.

### KICK THE BAD HABITS

• **"Help! I can't get off the couch..."** We're all guilty of this. Settling down in front of the TV and – ironically – being too tired to get up and go to bed. Set an alarm for 30 minutes before you want to be in bed so that you have a prompt to start your bedtime routine. You've really got to be firm with yourself. Keep a time in your head so that you know not to start watching the next episode of that addictive boxset.

- **"A nice glass of red will help me sleep ..."** Whilst alcohol will make you feel sleepy, too much before bedtime will detract from the quality of your sleep. Try to avoid alcohol (and coffee) before bed.

- **"I just want to check my social media ..."** Not only does this always drain more time than you expect, experts recommend avoiding screens before bedtime. The 'blue light' in screens suppresses melatonin production – the hormone that helps you sleep. Try to stop using devices two hours before you go to sleep.

## MAKE YOUR BEDROOM SLEEP-FRIENDLY

There are quick and simple changes you can make to create a greater feeling of calm in your bedroom. Start with colour. The most soothing bedroom colours are lavender, light grey, soft green, pale blue and deep blue. These colours encourage a cosy and calm ambience, reduce stress and anxiety and promote relaxation. A clean bedroom is also key – especially if you suffer from allergies. Aim to reduce the number of dust-gathering knick-knacks you have and keep surfaces clear to make your surroundings more soothing on the eye. You don't need to go completely minimal though – include a few well-placed items in your sanctuary that you find beautiful or that evoke warm memories.

# Go Green

Have you considered that you can do more than just change your life in 24 hours ... you can change the world! Well, start to at least ...

Sadly, when it comes to saving the world, you can't make the huge changes that governments need to implement. However, you can start with small changes in your life that, combined with a growing movement of people doing the same, all contribute to make a big impact.

## GOALS

- Devise a plan to make your life more environmentally friendly and save money.
- Make simple swaps and changes you can implement straight away.

### PLASTIC (ISN'T FANTASTIC)

Every day, approximately eight million pieces of plastic pollution find their way into the world's oceans. You can minimise the future damage now by recycling, reusing and choosing not to contribute:

- Stop using single-use plastics (e.g. straws, takeaway coffee cups). Buy a coffee cup that can be refilled.
- Keep a bag to hand that you can whip out when shopping rather than use a new plastic bag.

- Buy your fruit and veg loose rather than packaged in plastic. If you can't do this at your grocery store, try a local market (chances are the produce there will be cheaper too). Many stores can put purchases like meat in a reusable container you provide rather than their own plastic packaging.
- Buy goods in boxes rather than plastic – cardboard is easier to recycle.

## SAVE WATER, SAVE THE WORLD

- Keep showers short – every minute spent in a power shower uses up to 17 litres of water.
- Only put your washing machine or dishwasher on with a full load. (A full load in a dishwasher uses less water than washing-up by hand.)
- Replace your old-style, single flush toilet with a modern dual-flush system and save around 7 litres of water per flush.
- Fix that leaky tap. And stop leaving the tap running when you brush your teeth.

## EATING GREEN

- Switch to organic and fair trade where you can. A little pricier but you can save in other areas ...

- Get creative with leftovers. And if you do have food waste, compost it.
- Start growing your own. You don't need a lot of space even if you're in an apartment.
- Buying local not only supports small, local producers but will reduce the number of miles food travels to reach your table, cutting back on fuel consumption and emissions.
- Meat is the most resource-intensive of foods and eating less of it has a huge impact. If you're a meat eater, try cutting out a serving of meat each week.

## SAVE YOUR ENERGY

- Switch your energy supplier to one that's 100% renewable.
- Don't leave appliances on standby – they may not be 'on' but they're still using energy.
- Turn your thermostat down – even turning it down by one degree makes a difference.
- If you're buying a new appliance, replace it with one with a high energy-efficiency rating.
- Get into the habit of turning off lights when you leave a room. Switch your old lightbulbs for energy-efficient Compact Fluorescent Lamps (CFLs) and Light Emitting Diodes (LEDs).

# Quit Your Job

Handing in your notice: not a decision to be taken lightly. However, it's a move that, orchestrated properly, can have an incredibly positive impact on your life.

If your current job is troubling you, then it could be time for a change. Of course, a job equals security so you should always take any decision to move on seriously and plan it well. Chances are you've been deliberating for a while so give yourself 24 hours to focus and put a plan in place.

**GOALS**
- Leave your job for the right reasons and be in control of the situation.
- Plan those all-important next steps.
- Move forward without putting yourself at risk financially.

## WHY DO YOU WANT TO QUIT?

We all have awful days at work when we just want to leave and never return. However, leaving your job on a whim is rarely a good idea. Make a list of the reasons why you want to quit and set out all the pros and cons:

- **"I love my job but someone or something is making it miserable."** Who can you speak to about this? Ask yourself if it's fair to be forced to leave a job you enjoy.

- **"I want to try something else."** I thought this was the right job for me, but I feel unhappy and unfulfilled.
- **"I have a dream I want to pursue."** I want to travel the world. I want to retrain for a new career. I want to care for my children.
- **"My job is affecting my mental and physical health."** I need to get out of this job to protect my health.

### HANDING IN YOUR NOTICE

Tempting as it might be to quit with a flourish, do it in a way that doesn't lose you respect or your dignity. Don't forget, you're likely to be working out a notice period so avoid making your remaining time difficult. Likewise, you'll regret burning bridges when you ask for a reference! Have a plan of what you're going to say and replicate it clearly in a letter. Honesty is good, especially if your feedback might improve life for your colleagues. Be aware of what's in your contract – what is your notice period? What pay are you entitled to?

### PREP YOUR NEXT STEPS

Have an action plan in place. Dreams are wonderful but make sure they can become a reality before you give up a steady salary. Can you afford to travel around the world? Are you qualified to apply to train in a new career? People will take you more seriously if you've planned ahead and you may need to rely on their support. Put the wheels in motion for your next steps well in advance of handing in your notice to make the transition faster and less financially precarious.

### IF YOU'VE NOT GOT A JOB LINED UP ...

There are some situations where you might not have an alternative in place, for example, where your job is seriously affecting your physical and/or mental health. Get advice on your rights – if you're suffering and your employer hasn't helped resolve it, you may be entitled to compensation. Speak to someone close to you about what is happening and build your support network. It may be that you need to temporarily call on family or friends for financial assistance so make sure they understand fully what's going on in advance.

# Share a Problem

'A problem shared is a problem halved.' Never have truer words been said. It's okay not to be okay and it's okay to ask for help. No one is an island.

Are you struggling with a worry that's affecting your physical and mental well-being? It might be about work, yourself, a relationship, or even the state of the world. Regardless of whether it's big or small, sharing it with someone else and asking for support is daunting, but also incredibly valuable. The other person may not be able to solve the problem for you so don't expect that. What they can do is help you to find a solution and a way forward. They can support you by simply being at your side and holding your hand, literally if need be. Don't ever think that it's hopeless or that nothing can help you. There is always hope, so be courageous and reach out to someone. It will change your life.

**GOALS**
- Accept that you don't need to deal with everything by yourself.
- Reach out to someone else to share a problem that is troubling you.
- Move from a feeling of isolation to one of hope and positivity.

## REACH OUT

What's stopping you from talking to someone? It could be that you feel embarrassed or ashamed. Perhaps you think you'll look bad in the eyes of someone you love. The fact is that if someone loves and respects you, they'll be there for you whatever the problem. Choose someone to speak to that you really trust, who you know will treat what you tell them in confidence. Be bold – the weight that will be lifted off your shoulders is well worth the risk you take in opening up.

## WHAT WILL YOU GAIN?

- The benefit of someone else's perspective, which will give you a sense of perspective.
- Break free of the sense of isolation you're feeling.
- The comfort and security of knowing that someone else has your back.
- Release the pressure of keeping worries internalised before you reach melting point.

## IF YOU CAN'T TALK TO SOMEONE YOU KNOW ...

If you really don't feel able to speak to a friend, family member or colleague, that's okay. Sometimes it's easier to open up to a stranger and it's just as beneficial. There are helplines available with people waiting to support, listen and signpost you to additional help, and many offer text and email services too if you don't want to speak over the phone. You can also get in touch with a local counselling service and arrange an initial session. It's really important to use a counsellor you feel comfortable with so don't be afraid to try different ones until you find one that clicks.

## REMEMBER – YOU ARE NOT ALONE

Don't try and deal with a problem yourself. However tough things might seem, remember that you are *never* alone. There is no problem that's too big to resolve. Keeping it tucked inside will just make it seem bigger and less manageable. As with anything major in life, making the decision to take control rather than be controlled is huge and can be scary. Believe in yourself and, however hard it is, muster up the courage to talk to someone. It will be the best thing you've ever done.

95

This edition published in 2019
By SJG Publishing, HP22 6NF, UK

Author: Helen Redding
Cover design: Milestone Creative
Contents design: Seagulls

ISBN: 978-1-911517-96-2

Printed in China

10  9  8  7  6  5  4  3  2  1